Buddha and the Art of Money Management

Table of Contents

Chapter 1. Introduction

Discover the serenity within the storm of numbers, calculations, and financial stress as we unearth the ancient wisdom of the Buddha in managing money. This special report, 'Buddha and the Art of Money Management,' promises to guide you on an enlightened path towards financial wellness and peace. Its unique fusion of time-honored precepts of Buddhism with modern money management techniques will enable you to harness the tranquility of mindfulness, translate it into your daily financial decisions, and move towards abundance with grounded grace. Intended for every individual seeking to balance their spiritual growth with fiscal responsibility, this report beautifully simplifies the complex world of finance. Every page brings spiritual and economic harmony closer than ever. Acquire not only an enriched understanding of financial planning but also savor the peace that follows mindful money management. Dive in now and begin this heartening journey towards a Buddha-approved financial future!

Chapter 2. The Principle of Mindfulness in Money Management

Mindfulness, a term that holds profound significance in Buddhist philosophy, refers to an observant and non-judgmental state of mind. In essence, it suggests being in the 'now,' fully conscious of the present moment while accepting its entirety. When applied to money management, this principle can illuminate your path towards financial peace, offering an alternative way to conceptualize and interact with your personal finances.

2.1. Understanding Mindfulness

Fundamentally, mindfulness encourages you to be completely aware of your current state and the world around you, cultivating an accepting approach toward your experiences. In the context of managing money, becoming truly aware of your current financial situation is the first crucial step. To do this, take an inventory of your income, assets, liabilities, expenses, and financial goals. Maintain a non-judgmental stance while analyzing your economic realities. That is, don't indulge in self-blame or guilt regardless of what your current situation entails. Practice reflection, not reaction, to encourage a healthy relationship with your finances.

2.2. Mindful Spending

Economically, being mindful translates to spending your hard-earned money on items and experiences that add true value to your life. In mindful spending, the emphasis is on quality, not quantity. Rather than getting swayed by impulsive purchasing decisions driven by marketing tactics or societal expectations, you take the time to evaluate whether the intended expenditure aligns with your values and contributes towards your happiness and well-being.

Buying mindlessly feeds into a vicious cycle: spending that leads to short-lived pleasure, followed by buyer's remorse, which invariably results in more impulsive purchases to counteract the regret. The concept of mindful spending, in contrast, encourages conscious consumption and promotes effective wealth accumulation.

2.3. The Intervention of Compassion

Buddhist principles advocate compassion and generosity towards others. Applying these virtues in financial management implies wisely utilizing your resources to create positive impacts on the lives of others. This doesn't necessarily mean extravagant charitable contributions; even small actions, if driven by genuine empathy and love, can contribute to collective prosperity.

2.4. Financial Planning with Equanimity

Equanimity, often praised in Buddhism, is maintaining mental composure irrespective of life's ups and downs. This tenet holds particular value for those who invest. Financial markets are dynamic, ever-fluctuating realms affected by countless external factors. With equanimity, you can observe these market variations without panic, regardless of the circumstances.

It's essential to develop a well-thought-out investment strategy and stick to it, irrespective of the market conditions. Don't let fear or greed drive your financial decisions. Instead, keep track of market patterns and analyze your investments routinely, making mindful adjustments when necessary.

2.5. Simplifying Financial Life

Buddha's teachings often emphasize minimizing desire and the importance of simplicity. In finance, this could signify decluttering your portfolio, simplifying your investments, and avoiding needless debt accumulation.

Frequently, people tend to maintain unnecessary accounts, redundant policies, and multiple loans that render their financial lives complicated. Simplifying your financial life doesn't merely make it easier to manage, but often increases its efficiency by eliminating hidden charges and taxes linked with multiple instruments.

2.6. The Power of Gratitude

Buddhist philosophy places immense importance on the act of gratitude - it builds contentment, propels happiness, and cultivates a positive mindset. Express gratitude for what you have, and for your ability to manage it. Repeat this practice daily and watch your relationship with money transform.

Achieving financial wellness doesn't demand you to amass huge wealth. Rather, it's about making peace with what you have, and effectively managing and growing your resources to lead a secure, contented life. Mindfulness stands at the crux of it all; it's in acknowledging your present while making intelligent decisions for your financial future. So, begin your journey of mindful money management today, and stride towards a Buddha-approved financial future.

Chapter 3. The Middle Path: Balancing Spending and Saving

In an era dominated by the erratic duality of either extravagant spending or excessive saving, the concept of a 'middle path' might seem almost out of place. However, this is where Buddhism does its magic, teaching us to walk the harmonious path between these extremes---one that lays the foundation for a steady, serene, and sustainable financial future.

3.1. Understanding The Middle Path

In the context of financial management, the 'Middle Path' refers to an enlightened approach to navigating monetary affairs. It calls us to understand our relationship with money and to differentiate between our 'wants' and 'needs'. In doing so, it empowers us to find equilibrium between the opposing forces of spending and saving and arrive at a state of financial well-being.

To navigate this balanced path, it's critical to understand our relationship with money. We must acknowledge both the abundance and the scarcity, believing in the potential to generate wealth while being aware of the limitations of resources. A mindful recognition of our financial circumstances aids in cultivating an attitude of balance and moderation.

3.2. Balance Wants and Needs

At the heart of the Middle Path lies the ability to distinguish 'wants' from 'needs.' Needs are life necessities, like food, shelter, and clothing. Wants, on the other hand, are desires for luxury; non-essential goods and services. This differentiation serves as an essential guide in our fiscal journey, shaping our spending habits and saving plans.

It is paramount to mindfully assess your expenditure, maintaining your focus on fulfilling your needs. While it's natural to desire luxuries in life, overspending on trivial pursuits can lead to financial stress and dissatisfaction. Therefore, practice restraint and moderation, not denial or suppression, of wants.

3.3. Moderation, Not Denial

In the journey of mindful spending, it's vital to avoid the pitfall of austerity. Following the Middle Path does not imply denying oneself of all comforts for the sake of frugality. Instead, it emphasizes the conscientious identification of false necessities and unnecessary luxuries, fostering an attitude of 'enough.'

At every step of this journey, remember to reward yourself judiciously as an act of self-love and acceptance. Measure these rewards not by their financial costs but by the joy and fulfillment they bring to your life.

3.4. The Act of Mindful Saving

Saving is the foundation of financial well-being. While it's crucial to meet one's current needs, preparing for future requirements is equally important. The Middle Path encourages maintaining an equilibrium between present consumption and future savings.

Practicing conscious saving requires reviewing your income and expenses regularly, identifying opportunities to save, and ensuring your future financial safety. It involves setting apart a portion of your income regularly and investing it wisely to create wealth over the long term.

Explore various saving and investment avenues, such as mutual funds, stocks, bonds, or real estate, based on your financial goals, risk tolerance, and timeline. This diversified approach helps to spread risk and increase the potential for generating sustainable wealth.

3.5. Budgeting: Navigating Between Spending and Saving

Buddhism teaches that just as each individual is unique, so too is their path to financial equilibrium. It's here that budgeting plays a significant role, serving as a roadmap to guide, direct, and balance spending and saving.

Creating a mindful budget involves listing income sources, enumerating necessary expenses, and allocating funds for saving and discretionary spending. This is not a one-time exercise but a continuous process involving regular updates and adjustments as per changing circumstances.

3.6. Embrace Simplicity

One of the most powerful tools in following the Middle Path in money management is embracing simplicity. Simplifying lifestyle, needs, and desires can help in reducing financial stress and clutter. It can foster peace and contentment.

A simple lifestyle does not equate to austerity, nor does it mean giving up on your desires. It means choosing to focus on the essentials and deriving joy from these, letting go of the unnecessary extras that often cloud our true needs and spirit.

All things considered, the Middle Path's wisdom doesn't merely apply to one's fiscal life but instead extends to every aspect of existence. It asks us to practice mindfulness and awareness in every decision we make, to appreciate the abundance of this moment while being adequately prepared for the future. By learning to navigate between spending and saving, we not only enhance our financial well-being but also step towards a more serene and content life. Embrace this path to find prosperity not just in your wallet but also in your heart and soul.

Chapter 4. The Four Noble Truths of Personal Finance

The first aspect to take into account when beginning our journey in personal finances is understanding The Four Noble Truths from Buddhist teachings. Often called the truth of suffering (Dukkha), the truth of the cause of suffering (Samudaya), the truth of the end of suffering (Nirodha) and the truth of the path that leads to the end of suffering (Magga), these four truths have profound implications on how we manage our resources if we take the time to understand and apply them.

4.1. The Truth of Suffering (Dukkha) in Personal Finance

Often, as individuals, we are trapped in a cycle of financial suffering. This could come in many forms such as incurring high debts, dealing with unexpected expense, dissatisfaction with income, or worry about retirement funds. Ignorance about personal finance or insufficient monetary resources can intensify any financial discomfort and suffering.

What we need to realize is that this financial suffering (Dukkha) is a part of life, just as ups and downs are a common part of our existence. Acknowledging the presence of a problem is the first empowering step towards a solution. With complete acceptance, we can then start to implement changes to alleviate our financial distress.

4.2. The Truth of the Cause of Suffering (Samudaya) in Personal Finance

Looking beyond the surface, we must scratch to the root cause of our financial issues. The second Noble Truth, Samudaya, provides a perspective that suffering arises from attachment and desire. In the realm of personal finance, this can be attributed to unmanaged desires and uncontrolled spending habits, an attachment to materialistic comforts and luxury goods, disregard for future needs, or an unbalanced approach to money management.

Undeniably, attachment and greed play a substantial role in causing financial distress. It might not be our wrong decisions that have put us in a tough spot but rather the inability to control our desires. Therefore, recognizing and facing our attachments is crucial to prevent further financial suffering.

4.3. The Truth of the End of Suffering (Nirodha) in Personal Finance

While the first two truths may seem to paint a grim picture, with the third Noble Truth, Nirodha, respite arises. This truth promises that it is indeed possible to end this financial suffering. To accomplish this, we must reach a point of contentment where our needs are adequately met without giving rise to greed or insatiable wanting.

Achieving a state of financial contentment does not mean possessing a large bank balance or earning a hefty salary. Instead, it refers to having sufficient funds to meet our needs, save for the future, and be capable of surviving any unexpected financial blows. Financial Nirodha, thus, reflects a state of financial wellness where we live within our means, not obliged by anyone, and capable of handling unforeseen financial mishaps with wisdom and without anxiety.

4.4. The Truth of the Path Leading to the End of Suffering (Magga) in Personal Finance

The final Noble Truth, Magga, presents us with a path to end suffering. In terms of personal finance, it is about cultivating comprehensive money management strategies that align with our individual needs, goals, and financial situation.

This path could involve financial discipline, budgeting, mindful spending, regular saving, and prudent investing. This might also include you setting both short-term and long-term financial goals, educating oneself about financial tools and products, or seeking professional help, if necessary.

Making conscious efforts to navigate through this path of financial wellness might seem daunting initially, but with persistence and mindfulness, it will eventually lead us to financial Nirodha, thereby helping us end our financial suffering.

Aligning these Four Noble Truths with personal finance illuminates the path to financial wellness, harmony, and peace. As we embark on this journey, we should remember that the goal here is not to build immense wealth. But rather, it is about reaching a state where money no longer causes suffering and anxiety. After all, isn't that what we're all seeking in our quest to manage our money effectively - peace of mind? The Buddha's wisdom can help us acquire that balance—and keep it.

Chapter 5. Understanding Desires versus Needs: The Art of Letting Go

In the pursuit of mindful money management, we explore a fundamental concept - desire versus need. This distinction is vital in the thoughtful navigation of financial decisions. Understanding and applying the philosophies of Buddhism to this concept can provide profound clarity and aid in managing finances with tranquility and grace.

5.1. Defining Desires and Needs

Before understanding the contrast between desires and needs, it's crucial to define them. Needs represent the essentials. They are absolute necessities for our survival and wellness. Needs include shelter, food, clothing, healthcare, and even social interaction. On the other hand, desires depict the non-essential wants. They are craved for their ability to enhance our current standard of living or satisfaction but are not vital to survive or thrive.

In this context, the goal is not to suppress or demonize desires but to understand their place and purpose. Buddhism encourages us to identify and acknowledge our desires. The teachings of the Middle Way, a core theory in Buddhism, suggest striving for a balanced path. It asks us not to indulge in overspending due to unchecked materialistic desires nor live in unnecessary austerity by disregarding all desires.

5.2. The Role of Awareness

The key to distinguishing between needs and desires lies in

heightened awareness, a principle central to Buddhism. Mindfulness encourages us to look inward and understand the root cause of our desires versus actual needs. Practicing mindfulness within our money management can lead to sustainable financial wellness.

A common method for nurturing this mindfulness is through meditation. The stillness and self-reflection experienced during meditation can help untangle the webs of complex feelings of needs and desires, leading to clarity.

5.3. The Impermanence of Desires

Buddhist teaching proclaims anitya or impermanence, acknowledging the transient nature of things, including desires. This understanding encourages us to let go of the attachment to ephemeral pleasures. In the context of money management, realizing the fleeting nature of material possessions can guide us towards financial prudence.

We live in an era of consumerism, where various external sources continually create and fuel desires. Acknowledging the impermanence of these desires can help us make financially sound decisions. An understanding that satiating a temporary desire might not lead to prolonged happiness can prevent us from impulsive purchases driven by momentary wants, thus ensuring better control over finances.

5.4. Application to Money Management

Comprehending the distinction between desires and needs could profoundly affect your financial decisions, leading to mindful money management. The implementation of this understanding can take two primary forms:

Firstly, prioritizing needs over desires can ensure the adequate allocation of resources to what is essential. By taking care of our essential needs first, we establish a secure foundation, which can then be built upon.

Secondly, mindful recognition, examination, and evaluation of desires can promote conscious spending. Upon feeling a desire to make a purchase, pause, and reflect upon it. Is this a transient want or a need that contributes to your wellbeing? This awareness can reduce impulsive spending, aid in accumulation and investment, and promote financial peace and stability.

5.5. Budgeting: The Middle Way

Translating Buddha's Middle Way into money management could mean creating a balanced budget that neither represses nor pampers our desires. A practical starting point is to categorize our expenditure into needs, wants, savings, and donations. In this way, Buddhism's essence of compassion also gets a place in our finance.

In conclusion, understanding and distinguishing between desires and needs from a Buddhist perspective offers us a clear path for mindful and balanced money management. This art of letting go promotes financial responsibility while fostering the peace attributed to Buddhist teachings. Every step taken with mindful consideration brings us closer to achieving balance between spiritual growth and fiscal responsibility, moving towards a life of abundance in both spiritual and financial terms. By integrating these practices into our daily lives, we can enrich not only our financial futures, but also embark on a journey of growth and personal development.

Chapter 6. The Ethical Earnings: Money and Right Livelihood

Driven by curiosity, you have immersed yourself into the potent fusion of time-honored precepts of Buddhism and the intricate world of personal finance. The essence of Buddhism, around which this divine wisdom revolves, teaches us to lead a lifestyle endowed with moral, mindful, and meditative attributes. As we delve deeper into this journey, we knock on the door of the Noble Eightfold Path, a guiding framework that represents the core teachings of Buddha. Out of these eight principles, 'Right Livelihood' is one that strongly applies to financial management. Throughout this chapter, we explore the dimension of Right Livelihood in the context of personal finance, primarily focusing on ethical earnings.

6.1. Ethical Earnings: An Introduction

Basing our financial conduct on ethical grounds is a concept deeply embedded in Buddhism. This principle of ethical earnings corresponds to Right Livelihood, the one precept among the eight of Buddhism's Noble Eightfold Path that focuses on ethics in financial matters. It delicately integrates the moral circumference that defines how we earn and manage our money. Thus, when conversing about earning ethically, it becomes imperative to understand its fundamentals.

Ethical earnings necessarily mean securing an income in a way that neither harms oneself nor others. This way of earning promotes a sense of joy and pride in our labors, an approach that allows our work to contribute positively to our spiritual progress. Right

Livelihood, therefore, refuses to endorse occupations contributing to discomfort, harm, or suffering for oneself or others.

6.2. Synthesis of Right Livelihood and Personal Finance

Secular worldviews often position wealth and spiritual growth at odds, but Buddhism refutes this dichotomy. Buddhism emphasizes moral integrity and compassion, principles which find profound resonance in financial management when rooted in ethics. The synthesis of Right Livelihood and personal finance can be considered wholesome when the wealth accumulated neither contradicts the moral fabric nor exploits others for personal gain.

When applied to today's financial world, Right Livelihood encourages transparency, accountability, and morality. It implies a refusal to profiteer from activities that could harm others - discrediting the reckless pursuit of profits without social accountability.

6.3. Workplace and Right Livelihood

The concept of Right Livelihood is not confined to merely choosing a profession that complies with ethical norms. It also emphasizes maintaining an ethical approach within the chosen profession. This might involve seeking fair business practices, refusing bribery or dishonest gains, promoting equality, and ensuring a healthy working environment devoid of any form of oppression.

One can deepen their understanding of Right Livelihood by observing the Five Precepts of Buddhism, which prohibit killing, stealing, sexual misconduct, false speech, and intoxication. Consequently, any profession involving these negative actions directly or indirectly is considered to be in violation of Right Livelihood.

6.4. Investing Mindfully

Right Livelihood, when expanded to investments, advocates mindful investing. This philosophy invites us to consider not just the financial rewards but also how our investments impact the broader ecosystem. Consequently, individuals must invest in businesses that work in line with ethical principles while producing profits.

Mindful investors carefully scrutinize potential business investments for ethical operations, taking into consideration various factors such as environmental conservation, social responsibility, and corporate governance, often referred to collectively as ESG investing.

6.5. Right Livelihood for Personal Growth

While we perceive Right Livelihood primarily as a guide on how to earn, it plays a much deeper role in promoting personal growth. Ethical earnings garnered through right livelihood nourishes our soul, transforming work from a source of financial stability into an uplifting experience that enriches our life, enabling us to grow as fulfilled, well-rounded individuals. It further fuels a sense of purpose, providing economic benefits while contributing positively to the world around us.

As we wind up this chapter, remember the essence of Right Livelihood rests not so much on what we attain as how we attain it. By promoting ethical earnings, Buddhism teaches us that wealth and spirituality can coexist harmoniously, setting us on the path towards personal and collective prosperity. This approach to money management assures lasting financial peace, demonstrating that financial wellness and spiritual health are indeed two sides of the same coin. Adopting the principles of Right Livelihood in our professional and financial life, hence, promises a serene journey towards financial abundance and spiritual enlightenment.

Chapter 7. Financial Karma: Every Action Has a Financial Consequence

The concept of Karma has been an integral part of Buddhist philosophy for centuries. Karma, in its simplest form, suggests that every action has a corresponding consequence. Beyond a spiritual context, this principle bears a surprising relevance to money management. At the heart of this chapter is the belief that every financial decision we make, no matter how insignificant it might seem, carries weight and casts ripples into our fiscal future.

7.1. Understanding Financial Karma

Financial Karma revolves around the principle that every financial action we undertake leads to a chain of reactions. Spend frivolously without a thought for saving, and you'll end up in debt. Invest wisely and patiently, and you may enjoy financial growth and stability.

Put simply, your financial status at any given moment is not random. Instead, it represents the accumulation of all your past financial decisions, habits, actions and reactions. This concept works in parallel with the Buddhist law of Karma, wherein every action sows the seed for a future consequence, whether good or bad. The goal here, therefore, becomes one of mindful money management - ensuring our financial actions today lead to positive financial consequences in the future.

7.2. The Law of Cause and Effect in Finances

The Buddhist law of cause and effect, when applied to finances, essentially underscores the intricate relationship between our actions and the resultant fiscal outcomes.

1. Saving versus Spending It begins with understanding the difference between saving and spending. Spend money today and it's gone tomorrow. But save and invest it wisely, and it comes back to you multiplied. The latter is how wealth is cultivated and preserved.

2. Risk versus Reward Just as in life, in finance too, courage is rewarded. The well-known concept of 'higher risk equals higher reward' is reflective of this. However, it's essential to balance our risk-taking propensity with prudence, investing only in assets we truly understand.

3. Mindfulness versus Mindlessness Mindful spending and investing, characterized by careful research and thoughtful decision-making, tends to yield positive results. Conversely, mindless or impulsive financial behaviors usually lead to undesirable predicaments like debt, bankruptcy, or extreme stress.

Good financial Karma, at its core, means aligning our actions today to cultivate a fruitful tomorrow.

7.3. Mindful Spending and Investing

Intention and awareness are two foundational pillars supporting Buddhist teachings. They drive us towards being mindful about our actions in relation to ourselves and others. When it comes to financial management, the application of mindful spending and investing is built on these two pillars.

Being mindful with money involves knowing when and where we spend or invest our resources. It's about conscious decision-making, avoiding impulsive purchases, refraining from unnecessary expenses, and having a clear understanding of our financial goals.

Similarly, mindful investing is not about making quick money or trying to 'beat the market'. Instead, it requires deep understanding, consistent diligence, and unwavering patience as we allow our investments to grow and compound over time.

7.4. Cultivating Positive Financial Karma

Gaining financial clarity and cultivating positive financial Karma entails four essential steps:

1. Understanding Your Financial Behaviors: Reflect on your past and existing financial habits. Keep those that serve you, change those that don't.

2. Fostering Financial Discipline: Inculcate a disciplined approach to managing money. Draft a realistic budget and stick to it, save diligently, and invest wisely.

3. Prioritizing Debt Repayment: Don't let debt overshadow your finances. Strategize to pay your dues on time to avoid liabilities compounding and getting out of hand.

4. Setting Long-Term Financial Goals: Define what financial success looks like to you, make a plan, and stay committed to it no matter what.

By conscientiously following these steps, we align ourselves towards solid financial health and cultivate positive financial Karma.

7.5. The Ripple Effect of Financial Karma

Once we activate our positive financial Karma, its ripple effect extends beyond our bank balance. Fiscally responsible and mindful behaviors can positively influence our overall well-being, reduce stress, and improve our relationships. Choices made with mindfulness and wisdom bring us closer to achieving long-term financial stability and enduring peace of mind.

In essence, understanding and applying the principle of financial Karma is a powerful means to navigate the stormy sea of fiscal obligations. With the wisdom of Buddha guiding us, we can indeed balance our financial and spiritual life. Let's cultivate good financial Karma together, fostering wealth and well-being in harmony with our cherished principles.

Chapter 8. The Eightfold Path to Financial Freedom

To embark on a journey towards financial freedom, let's explore the principles and teachings of Buddhism to guide our voyage to economic prosperity. This Eightfold Path for Financial Freedom offers an enlightening perspective for mindful money management as inspired by the wisdom of Buddha.

8.1. Understanding Right View

Firstly, it is essential to have the Right View. This doesn't refer to subscribing to any dogmatic economic principles but, encouraging you to understand the nature of financial concepts, their interconnectedness, the morality of money, and our role in the economic world. Seeing that our financial choices feed into the larger economic ecosystem illuminates our path.

Everything is interconnected. Even individual economic activities are expressions of universal ones. When you buy a coffee, you aren't just exchanging money for a drink. You're partaking in global economic activities – supporting farmers in one part of the world, contributing to the logistics industry, supporting the local economy, and more. This interconnectedness implies that our financial dealings have larger, rippling impacts. We must strive to comprehend these connections and how our actions feed into them.

8.2. Practicing Right Intention

We must set a vibrant intent for our financial journey, both practically and ethically, by committing to our economic growth without harming others or ourselves. It means practicing discernment in our economic engagements and refraining from getting entangled in money-making schemes that may harm others.

A right intention would be aiming for financial prosperity while also ensuring that we uphold values like honesty, integrity, and compassion. After all, wealth isn't just measured in terms of material assets; it includes inner wealth of peace, happiness, and sense of purpose.

8.3. Implementing Right Speech

Right Speech in a financial context means honest and clear communication about our monetary matters. Oftentimes, money can be a subject of deceit and confusion. We need to ensure we are truthful in our monetary interactions with people around us.

Being genuine in our financial communications ensures trust and transparency. It's about saying, "I can't afford it," rather than going into debt due to societal pressures or maintaining a façade. It also revolves around communicating honestly with partners about money or admitting when we need financial help. Honesty, after all, is the currency that never devalues.

8.4. Embracing Right Action

Here, we translate our comprehensions into financial decisions. Right action means making informed, ethical, and beneficial financial moves. This involves being a mindful consumer, choosing to buy products that are not harmful - either to people or the planet.

Right action also includes practicing ethical investments and supporting businesses that align with our values. It's about supporting economic models and industries that reflect our values, thus becoming an agent of change in the economy.

8.5. Creating Right Livelihood

Right Livelihood involves earning money in a moral and ethical manner, without causing harm or distress to ourselves or others. Everyone has a right to earn money, but the means to accumulate it should not amplify distress to others.

Conscious business practices, green jobs, socially responsible investing, and fair trade are examples of right livelihood. It's about aligning our profession with our values, ensuring the way we earn money also serves a purpose beyond just survival.

8.6. Cultivating Right Effort

Cultivating the Right Effort reminds us that our financial journey is a marathon, not a sprint. It requires consistent effort and patience. Extricating ourselves from bad financial habits, paying off debts, accumulating wealth, all demand a level-headed, steady effort.

If you owe a large debt or are in a difficult financial situation, remember the wisdom in Buddhism: our present situation is the product of past actions but our future will be affected by what we do in the present. So, keep working with diligence and patience.

8.7. Developing Right Mindfulness

Right Mindfulness entails staying aware of our thoughts, actions, and decisions related to money. It involves noticing our money habits, good or bad, evaluating them, and learning from them.

Mindfulness can help us identify our unconscious money scripts and deal with issues like impulsive shopping or hoarding. By becoming aware of our money habits, we can work on creating healthier ones.

8.8. Embracing Right Concentration

Finally, Right Concentration suggests focused mental work. Creating a financial plan, budgeting, or troubleshooting a pressing financial issue all involve concentrated efforts.

Concentrated focus on our financial goals helps us avoid distractions that may steer us away from the path of financial freedom. Creating a vivid visualization of our financial goals and then working diligently to achieve them forms the essence of Right Concentration.

This newly unveiled path can become a lantern to guide you through tumultuous economic winds. It promises to enable you to pursue wealth and financial freedom holistically and ethically. So, set forth and embark on this spiritual journey of insightful financial enlightenment.

Chapter 9. Detachment from Material Wealth: Viewing Possessions Anonymously

Despite the escalating accumulation of material wealth in our contemporary world, it is important to understand and embrace the concept of detachment from materialistic possessions. Such an understanding is not a repudiation of wealth. Rather, it offers a profound perspective that allows us to experience wealth without it consuming our consciousness. In this context, we examine the idea of viewing possessions anonymously, abstracting material possessions from our self-identity, thereby cultivating non-attachment.

9.1. The Doctrine of Anatta

Buddhism expounds on the doctrine of Anatta, often translated as 'not-self'. The Buddha suggested that the root of suffering is a fundamental misunderstanding about the nature of the self. We mistakenly associate our identity to mutable, external phenomena; among them, our material possessions. The truth of Anatta challenges this misconception, highlighting the impermanence and interdependence of all things, including our own sense of self.

Disentangling ourselves from our possessions doesn't necessitate asceticism. Instead, the goal is to see material wealth for what it truly is—a collection of transient, interdependent phenomena that can provide comfort and convenience, but not lasting happiness or self-definition.

9.2. The Illusion of Ownership

"Who really owns anything?" This question forms a cornerstone of

Buddhist thinking about possessions. If we consider the principle of Anatta, we arrive at a startling truth - we own nothing. Our perceived control over external phenomena, including wealth, is temporary and capricious.

The notion of ownership is ingrained from a young age. Children are taught to respect each other's 'property', nurturing a possessive instinct that grows stronger with age. However, revisiting our understanding of ownership with our newly acquired Buddhist perspective, we see the value in redefining our relationship with material wealth.

Seeing wealth as an anonymous entity—a pool of resources that flows in and around us, but which does not belong to us—can bring enormous freedom. It relieves us of the burden of 'having', allowing us to focus on the joy of 'being'.

Practically, viewing money as a neutral tool rather than a personal possession enables us to make more rational and less emotionally charged financial decisions. We can better resist impulsive spending and cultivate a responsible and generous approach to managing wealth.

9.3. The Art of Detachment

Detaching from material wealth doesn't insinuate a lack of motivation for success or progress. Rather, it is an enlightened way of interacting with our possessions. Detachment is viewing our possessions unpossessively, a radical shift in perspective that can profoundly alter our interaction with material wealth.

Forming a detached relationship with our possessions helps in diffusing the potent emotional reactions either towards gain or loss. We are less likely to experience anxiety, greed, or resentment in connection to our finances. Instead, we can embrace an equanimous attitude; valuing wealth for the opportunities it affords, while retaining emotional stability irrespective of its presence or absence. Every financial gain or loss, every fulfilled or unfulfilled desire can then become lessons enlightening our path to financial wellness and peace.

Our financial decisions can also benefit from the objectivity inherent in detachment. Investing, for example, can be approached as a strategy with calculated risks and opportunities, rather than a stress-inducing gamble, weighed down by fears of material loss. Similarly, we can navigate financial hardships with greater resilience, viewing these as temporary conditions rather than defining our self-worth.

9.4. Gratitude and Generosity

Beyond the personal tranquility that detachment cultivates, lies a host of societal benefits. By viewing possessions anonymously, we can cultivate a sense of gratitude for the resources that come our way and generosity towards sharing them with others.

This new perspective can transform our relationship with consumption too. With a focus on mindful consumption, we can move away from excessive consumerism, reducing the burden on our planet while also fostering a more equitable social order. Moreover, by giving freely, we nurture a network of reciprocity, compassion, and shared prosperity.

9.5. Concluding Thoughts

It is important to remember that the path towards viewing possessions "anonymously" is not always easy. It requires consistent practice, self-awareness, and a willingness to challenge deep-seated beliefs about wealth and identity. However, the benefits are multi-fold - personal tranquility, more rational financial decision-making, and a generous, equitable perspective towards resource distribution.

Moving forward, let us apply the principles of Anatta, the illusion of ownership, the art of detachment, and the cultivation of gratitude and generosity to our interaction with material wealth. Each dollar spent or saved can then become a step towards an enlightened, Buddha-approved financial future.

Chapter 10. Meditation and Money: Mastering Patience in Investments

The intricate, intertwining paths of financial investment and Buddhist meditation may appear to contrast starkly at first glance. However, both require a deep sense of patience, a trait directly mastered through meditative practices.

In this context, let's explore how integrating meditation into your investment journey can foster the masterful patience needed to navigate the turbulent waves of the financial markets, ultimately leading to significant fiscal and personal growth.

10.1. Understanding the Essence of Patience

Firstly, it is crucial to understand what patience truly means within Buddhist teachings and in the world of investment. In Buddhism, patience is not merely a virtue but a form of wisdom. Inward patience involves developing an understanding, acceptance, and peace with ourselves, embracing our frailties along with our strengths. Outwardly, it manifests as the ability to accept life's situations without agitation.

Similarly, in investment decisions, patience means resisting the rush of quick returns and appreciating the slow, steady apprizing growth intrinsic to successful long-term investment. It is understanding that success in investing does not come overnight and involves perseverance in the face of market fluctuation.

10.2. Cultivating Patience through Meditation

How do we cultivate such patience? At the heart of Buddhism lies the practice of meditation, a tool to train the mind just as we train our bodies. In particular, mindfulness meditation involves focusing wholeheartedly on the current moment, accepting it without judgment: a direct way to nurture patience.

To begin, dedicate a set time daily for mindfulness meditation. Sit comfortably and focus on your breath, allowing thoughts to come and go without interaction or judgment. In practicing this, we learn to embrace each moment on its own, removing the anxiety of the past and the future - this in turn encourages patience within us.

Just like the practice of meditation strengthens with time, our investments too multiply with persistence and time in the market.

10.3. Translating Meditation to Investment Strategies

Can a meditative mindset indeed influence investment actions? Acknowledging this interconnection paves the way for more grounded investment decisions, encouraging long-term commitment over short-term, emotional reactions.

Take, for example, the initial panic ensuing market dips. A meditative mindset, cultivated from patience, will encourage calm, logical decisions rather than an impulsive selling reaction. Remembering our interaction (or lack thereof) with fleeting thoughts during meditation, we learn to view these market fluctuations as temporary.

On the flip side, during market highs, patience discourages rash decisions like aggressive buying. It maintains the understanding that not all peaks assure future growth, eliminating greed to make balanced decisions.

10.4. Temperament is Key in Investing

Warren Buffet, one of the most successful investors in the world, stated, "The stock market is a device for transferring money from the impatient to the patient." This statement illuminates the undeniable link between patience and successful investing.

A patient investor is akin to a meditator. Both understand the value of resilience, acceptance, and the ebbing and flowing nature of existence. Both know that turbulence is part of the journey and that rushing the process or reacting impulsively often leads to regrettable outcomes. By maintaining a calm demeanor in the midst of market volatility, patient investors are rewarded with successful returns over time.

10.5. Practical Ways to Incorporate Patience

1. Regular meditation: Begin or end your day with at least 15 minutes of meditation. This will help build a foundation for patience in all facets of life, investments included.

2. Diversification: Include a variety of assets in your portfolio. This not only reduces risk but also assures that some of your investments are likely to yield a good return over the long run.

3. Sustainability over speed: Resist get-rich-quick schemes; stick to sustainable growth strategies.

4. Education: Understand your investments deeply. Knowledge extracts fear and cultivates patience.

5. Financial Advisor: Seek counsel from a financial advisor. They maintain the emotional objectivity you might struggle with, rendering patient decisions more feasible.

10.6. Enduring Success

As a final point, this chapter emphasizes the importance of patience in both the financial and personal domains. Through meditative practices, not only are we equipped to cultivate this patience, but we are also granted a path to innately understanding the transient nature of the market's highs and lows. Combining these integrated disciplines in our investment journey guarantees success in finance and peace of mind.

With patience, we can endure market instabilities, confident in our belief of eventual growth. Investment success, much like enlightenment, is not a destination but a continually evolving journey, encouraging growth, patience, and ultimately, a fulfilling life enriched with tranquility and abundance.

Remember, wealth "flowered" from patient investment and mindful meditation practices promises not just monetary success, but also a rich, serene life that is at peace with its financial decisions, a life fully experienced and deeply understood.

Chapter 11. Attaining Nirvana: The Contentment of Financial Independence

Before diving into the intricate connect between religious enlightenment and financial independence, it is imperative to understand the terms in their unique and interrelated contexts. In Buddhism, Nirvana is the epitome of spiritual enlightenment - a state of perfect quietude, freedom, and highest happiness. Contrarily, financial independence represents the monetary state where your savings generate enough income for sustenance, minus active employment. The chapter sets to explore and intertwine these seemingly distinct pathways, leading to contentment.

11.1. The Intersection of Spiritual and Monetary Wealth

Finding a meeting point between Buddhist philosophies and economic abundance may seem a Herculean task due to their contrasting character. However, when we delve deeper, the junction becomes more evident. Wealth in Buddhism refers not solely to material gain but entails moral, mental, and spiritual richness. Financial independence, correspondingly, assigns worth beyond financial concerns, including freedom and peace. Their shared essence is striking - fulfillment not merely via possession but tied significantly to intangible, invaluable experiences and virtues.

11.2. Faith in the Principle of Cause and Effect

The concept of Karma forms a pivotal point in Buddhist teachings, wherein consequent effects arise from our actions. In the field of finance, this principle lives in budgeting and savings. When you save, it contributes to an effect - a steady growth of wealth, leading towards financial independence. Therefore, practicing financial prudence is akin to sowing good seeds, bearing bountiful results in the future.

11.3. Embracing Simplicity and Minimization

The teachings of the Buddha underscore the principle of reduction. This translates into finance as decluttering unnecessary expenses to focus on crucial and rewarding investments. It helps in trimming the hedonic treadmill that hitchhikes our financial growth with an increase in desires. Financial simplicity aids in the navigation towards wealth accumulation and serves as a steppingstone towards financial freedom.

11.4. Attaining the Middle Path in Finances

The Middle Path, a fundamental Buddhist tenet, advocates balance. In finance, it resonates with risk management. By diversifying investments and maintaining a balance between risk and return, we can maintain financial stability. This considered approach deters us from reckless endeavors while still encouraging growth-focused interventions.

11.5. Mindfulness and Conscious Spending

Mindfulness, a vital practice in Buddhism, can transform how we deal with money. By being mindful, deliberateness is introduced in our spending patterns, eliminating impulsive buying. This conscious consumption ensures money is directed towards utilities and investments bearing substantial emotional and financial returns, aiding in achieving financial independence.

11.6. Disentanglement from Material Attachments

Buddhist philosophy encourages detachment from material desires, helping us focus on our intrinsic needs over externally-influenced wants. A similar detachment in finance can prevent excessive consumption and encourage a frugal lifestyle. It simplifies financial decisions by aligning them with our true needs, fostering a stable journey towards economic freedom.

11.7. Compassionate Generosity and Its Rewards

Generosity is a Buddhist virtue that holds financial implications. When one practices giving – be it wealth, time, or skills, it nourishes gratitude within and radiates positive energy into the universe. Financially, it promotes healthy relations, induces a sense of contentment and sets up a virtuous cycle of give-and-take, ingratiating towards financial independence.

In conclusion, ironically, the path of Nirvana and the way to financial independence are not polar ends of a spectrum, but parallel journeys that reflect and feed each other. Each step towards financial independence doesn't stray you farther from spiritual enlightenment but rather, guides you to embody the teachings of Buddha in your daily financial decisions. Understanding and embracing the fusion of sages' wisdom with modern money management can bring about an enlightened approach to wealth and well-being. Witness the transformation that mindful money manners can bring and enjoy the contentment that is akin to Nirvana.